Maria Shkreli

All rights reserved.

No part of this publication may be reproduced, distributed, or transmitted in any form or by any means without prior written permission from the publisher, except for brief quotations used in professional reviews.

Title: The Cycle Breaker Method™

Employee Edition

A System for Communication, Boundaries, and Consistent Response

Author: Maria Shkreli

More information and related resources:

www.cyclebreakermethod.com

Publisher: Twentynine Publishing LLC

First Edition: April 2026

Printed in the United States of America

ISBN: 979-8-234-07298-6

Organizational Use Notice

The Cycle Breaker Method™ is designed to support individual and team-level application in everyday workplace interactions.

Employees and teams may use the method internally to improve communication, clarify expectations, and respond more consistently in professional environments.

Consistent use supports more stable and predictable interactions over time.

The method is intended to support professional communication, consistency, and workplace stability through practical application.

Use of Materials

All content, frameworks, and models within the Cycle Breaker Method™ are the intellectual property of Maria Shkreli.

This material may be used for internal reference and application.

It may not be:

- reproduced for external distribution
- modified or rebranded
- used commercially without written permission
- repackaged, reproduced, or presented as an original proprietary system

Organizational Implementation Inquires

Organizations or teams seeking further support in applying the method may contact:

For organizational inquiries:

maria@cyclebreakermethod.com

www.cyclebreakermethod.com

About the Author

Maria Shkreli, LMHC, is a licensed mental health counselor, author, and workplace behavioral consultant specializing in pattern recognition, interpersonal dynamics, and structured behavioral change.

She is the creator of the Cycle Breaker Method™, a pattern-based framework developed through years of clinical practice and real-world application. Her work focuses on identifying repeated interaction patterns and teaching structured responses that reduce conflict, strengthen boundaries, and improve consistency in both personal and professional environments.

Maria is the author of Breaking Cycles and Breaking Up with Toxicity, and the host of the podcast Breaking Up with Toxicity, where she explores behavioral patterns, relational dynamics, and systems that influence how people interact.

Her work is based on a simple but often overlooked reality:

Many problems do not persist because people are unwilling to change.

They persist because patterns are repeated without interruption.

Over time, unclear expectations, inconsistent responses, avoidance, and emotional reactivity begin to feel normal.

People adjust to the dysfunction instead of correcting it.

The Cycle Breaker Method™ was created to change t

Executive Summary

Workplace stability shapes your day-to-day experience at work.

When communication is clear, expectations are defined, and responses are consistent, work becomes more manageable, predictable, and less stressful.
When it is not, the same problems repeat.

Workplace patterns develop over time.
They are reinforced when situations are met with inconsistent or unclear responses.

This method is built on a simple principle:

Patterns become stable when responses become consistent.

Most workplace challenges are not isolated.
They are repeated patterns.

Why Workplace Situations Keep Repeating

Many workplace issues continue because:

- expectations are not clearly stated
- communication changes depending on the situation
- responses are inconsistent under pressure

Effort is often present.
Consistency is not.

The result is repeated confusion, miscommunication, and frustration.

What Actually Changes Your Experience at Work

Workplace patterns begin to shift when your responses become:

- clear
- direct
- consistent
- repeatable

Not occasionally.
Consistently.

What This Method Is

The Cycle Breaker Method™ is not about changing the workplace.
It is about changing how you respond within it.

Workplace patterns shift when responses become more clear, consistent, and predictable.

This method provides a structured way to:
- recognize repeated patterns
- communicate clearly
- reinforce boundaries
- respond consistently under pressure
- reduce repeated workplace issues

What This Changes

You do not control:
- other people's behavior
- leadership decisions
- workplace structure

You do control:
- your communication
- your boundaries
- your responses

That is where change begins.

What to Expect

At first, you may notice:
- situations feel uncomfortable
- responses feel unfamiliar
- others react differently

This does not mean the method is not working.

It means the pattern is being interrupted.

What Improves Over Time

With consistent application:
• communication becomes clearer
• expectations become more defined
• repeated issues decrease
• your role becomes more stable

Not because everything changes.
Because your responses become more consistent.

Final Principle

What you consistently allow becomes what you consistently experience.

How to Use This Book

This book is not meant to be read passively.
It is meant to be applied.

What This Book Is

This book is a practical guide to:

- recognizing workplace patterns
- improving communication
- reinforcing boundaries
- responding consistently under pressure

It is designed for real situations—not ideal conditions.

What This Book Is Not

This is not:

- a theory-based book
- a personality assessment
- a motivational guide

It does not focus on:

- diagnosing others
- changing the workplace environment

It focuses on one thing:

How you respond within it.

How to Approach This Book

Patterns change when responses change.

You do not need to apply everything at once.

Start with one area:

- communication
- expectations
- boundaries
- response under pressure

How to Use Each Section

For every situation:

- Identify the pattern
- Clarify what is happening
- Apply a consistent response
- Reinforce that response

The Goal

The goal is not perfection.
The goal is stability.

When your responses become consistent:

- When your responses become consistent
- expectations become clearer
- conflict is reduced
- outcomes become more predictable

Important Reminder

You do not control:

- other people
- how others respond

You control:

- your communication
- your boundaries

That is enough to change patterns.

Final Note Before You Begin

Not once.
Not occasionally.
Consistently.

Quick Start — Use This Today

If you are dealing with a difficult situation right now, start here:

1. Identify What Is Repeating

This is not a one-time issue.
What part of this situation feels familiar?

2. Pause Before Responding

Do not react immediately.

3. Clarify What Is Actually Happening

Separate:

- what was said
- what you assumed
- what is unclear

4. Apply a Clear Response

Focus on:

- clarity
- consistency

Example:
Instead of:
"I already explained this. I don't know why this keeps happening."

Say:
"Let's clarify expectations so this doesn't repeat."

5. Repeat the Same Response Next Time

Patterns change when your response becomes consistent.

Final Reminder

You do not need to fix the workplace.

You need to stabilize your response within it.

Introduction — Workplace Patterns and Your Role in Them

The Cycle Breaker Method™ is applied through consistent response within the Workplace Pattern Cycle.

The same misunderstandings.
The same frustrations.
The same unresolved conversations.

You are not just experiencing these patterns.

Every Response Matters

Every response you give either:

- reinforces the pattern
- interrupts it

How Workplace Patterns Develop

Workplace patterns develop through repetition.

EVENT
↓
INTERPRETATION
↓
RESPONSE
↓
REINFORCEMENT
↓
NORMALIZATION
↓
NEXT EVENT

Over time, these patterns shape:

Most employees focus on what happened.
Few focus on what was reinforced.

That is where patterns are created.

Your Role

You are not just responding to workplace dynamics.

Every response:

- reinforces
- interrupts

The Shift

Most people try to fix situations.
Professionals focus on responses.

Patterns become stable when responses become consistent.

What This Book Will Help You Do

- recognize repeated patterns
- respond more consistently
- reduce unnecessary conflict
- create more predictable outcomes

What This Changes

When your responses change:

- your interactions change
- your experience changes
- your outcomes improve

Closing

You do not need control over the workplace to improve your experience within it.
You need consistency in how you respond.

Pattern Reference — Unstable vs Stable Responses

Workplace stability develops through consistent response repeated over time.

Pattern Area	**Unstable Response**	**Stable Response**
Communication	emotional, long, unclear	clear, direct, neutral
Expectations	assumed, implied	stated, confirmed
Boundaries	inconsistent, avoided	defined, reinforced
Emotional Regulation	reactive, impulsive	measured, intentional
Pressure	inconsistent under pressure	consistent under pressure
Difficult Situations	avoided or escalated	addressed directly
Personal Patterns	automatic, repeated	recognized, interrupted

Point of Control

EVENT
↓
INTERPRETATION
↓
RESPONSE ← CONTROL POINT
↓
REINFORCEMENT
↓
NORMALIZATION
↓
NEXT EVENT

Section 1 — Understanding Workplace Patterns

The same conversations.
The same misunderstandings.
The same tension between the same people.

Not because the situation is identical—
but because the responses become predictable.

Professional growth begins when you recognize what repeats.

Workplace Pattern Model

EVENT
↓
INTERPRETATION
↓
RESPONSE ← CONTROL POINT
↓
REINFORCEMENT
↓
NORMALIZATION
↓
NEXT EVENT

Event → something happens
Interpretation → you assign meaning
Response → how you respond under pressure
Reinforcement → what your response allows
Normalization → what becomes "how things are"

Most people try to fix the event.
Professionals learn to stabilize the response.

Response Focus

- Correcting every misunderstanding
- Proving their point
- Forcing resolution

The method focuses on something different:

- Stabilizing communication
- Maintaining professional consistency
- Interrupting reactive patterns

Common Employee Mistake

Trying to fix the wrong part of the cycle:

- over-explaining
- reacting emotionally
- avoiding the issue
- hoping it changes

These responses do not break patterns.
They reinforce them.

What Actually Changes Patterns

Patterns change when responses change.

Not once.
Not occasionally.
Consistently.

Inconsistent response → confusion → instability
Consistent response → clarity → stability

Pause Before Responding

Before reacting, ask:

- What part of the cycle am I in?
- What response will reinforce this?
- What response will stabilize this?

You do not need to control the workplace to change your experience within it.

You need to understand the pattern developing —and respond differently, on purpose.

Recognizing Unstable Patterns Early

They appear as small moments:

- a conversation that feels slightly unclear
- an expectation that was not fully stated
- a response that changes depending on the situation

This is where patterns begin.

Most employees recognize patterns after they repeat.

At that point:

- frustration has already built
- responses have already become reactive
- the pattern has already been reinforced

The point of control is earlier than most people think.

Early Pattern Indicators

- communication feels inconsistent
- expectations are implied, not stated
- responses vary depending on pressure
- situations feel familiar but unresolved

These are not isolated issues.
They are early signs of a repeating pattern.

Professional Standard

Do not wait for repetition to confirm a pattern.
Recognize the structure early.

Quick Check

- Does this situation feel unclear or inconsistent?
- Has something like this happened before?
- Is the response changing depending on the situation?

Reset

Clarify early.
Respond consistently.
Do not wait for the pattern to fully develop.

Closing

Communication is where patterns become visible.

This is where consistency begins—either reinforcing instability or creating stability.

Workplace Pattern Quick Check

Check any that apply:

☐ Conversations often feel unclear or unresolved
☐ Expectations change depending on the person or situation
☐ Similar issues repeat with the same people
☐ Responses become emotional under pressure
☐ Boundaries are implied instead of clearly stated
☐ Communication changes depending on urgency or stress
☐ Problems are discussed repeatedly without resolution
☐ Responses vary instead of remaining consistent
☐ Frustration builds before concerns are clarified

Reflection

- Which pattern appears most often?

- Which response tends to reinforce it?

- What would a more stable response look like?

Section 2 — Communication That Reduces Conflict

Most workplace communication problems are not about what is said.
They are about how it is said, when it is said, and what it reinforces.

Most people assume communication is about expressing themselves.
In professional environments, communication is about influencing outcomes.

Communication Intent

Most employees communicate to:

- explain
- defend
- justify
- be understood

Professional communication focuses on:

- clarify
- stabilize communication
- reduce escalation
- reinforce expectations

Reactive vs Professional Communication

Reactive Communication

- emotional
- defensive
- over-explanatory
- inconsistent

Professional Communication

- clear
- direct
- neutral
- consistent

Where Communication Breaks Down

Communication becomes unstable when it is:

- unclear
- inconsistent
- emotionally driven
- overly detailed
- avoidant

This creates:

- confusion
- frustration
- repeated conflict
- tension

The Real Problem

Most employees change their communication based on:

- mood
- stress
- who they are speaking to

That inconsistency reinforces unstable patterns.

How Conflict Repeats

UNCLEAR MESSAGE
↓
MISINTERPRETATION
↓
EMOTIONAL RESPONSE
↓
DEFENSIVENESS
↓
REPEATED CONFLICT

What Stabilizes Communication

Stable communication has four characteristics:

- clear
- direct
- neutral
- consistent

Example Shift

Unstable:
"I didn't mean it like that, you're misunderstanding me..."

Stable:
"Let me clarify what I meant."

Unstable:
"This keeps happening and it's really frustrating..."

Stable:
"This has come up a few times. Let's clarify it directly."

Clarity reduces confusion.
Consistency reduces repetition.

Micro Scripts — Clear, Direct, Neutral

Use simple, repeatable languages:

- "Let me clarify what I meant."
- "This has come up a few times. Let's address it directly."
- "I want to make sure this is clear moving forward."
- "Let's make sure we're aligned before continuing."
- "Let's keep this focused and clear."
- "I've addressed this. I'm going to keep the response consistent."

Communication Control Point

Before responding, ask:

- Is this clear?
- Is this direct?
- Is this neutral?
- Would I say this the same way again?

If not, the response may be reinforcing instability.

Reset When Needed

If your response is:

- emotional → pause
- long → simplify
- defensive → reset
- unclear → clarify

What Most People Get Wrong

They assume:
more explanation = better communication

In reality:
more explanation can creates more confusion

Say less.
Mean it clearly.
Repeat it consistently.

When Communication Becomes Emotional

Do not:

- match the tone
- escalate
- over-explain

Instead:

- slow down
- clarify
- restate expectations

PAUSE
↓
CLARIFY
↓
STATE EXPECTATION
↓
STOP

You do not need perfect communication.
You need consistent communication.

That is what stabilizes the environment around you.

When Leadership Is Inconsistent

In many workplaces, communication is not consistent.

What is said in one situation may change in another.
Expectations may shift based on pressure, priorities, or leadership style.

This creates confusion—not necessarily because of lack of effort, but because of lack of stability.

Most employees adjust by:

- responding differently under pressure
- changing tone depending on who they are speaking to
- over-explaining in uncertain situations
- hesitating to be direct

This does not solve the problem.
It reinforces instability.

Professional Standard

Do not adjust your communication based on inconsistency.
Maintain stable communication despite it.

Quick Check

- Am I changing how I communicate depending on the situation?
- Am I over-adjusting to unclear or shifting expectations?
- Am I trying to match inconsistency instead of stabilizing it?

Reset

Clear.
Direct.
Neutral.
Consistent.

Professional Stability Pattern Check

Rate each statement based on how consistently it applies to you:
1 = Rarely
2 = Occasionally
3 = Sometimes
4 = Usually
5 = Consistently

Communication

- I communicate clearly under pressure. ____
- I keep my responses direct and neutral. ____
- I avoid over-explaining when frustrated. ____
- I clarify instead of assuming. ____

Expectations

- I confirm expectations before moving forward. ____
- I address confusion early. ____
- I restate expectations consistently. ____
- I avoid relying on implied understanding. ____

Boundaries

- I reinforce boundaries consistently. ____
- I avoid taking responsibility for unclear expectations. ____
- I remain professional even when others are reactive. ____
- I respond consistently across situations. ____

Emotional Response

- I pause before reacting emotionally. ____
- I recognize when pressure is affecting my communication. ____
- I avoid matching emotional tone. ____
- I reset instead of escalating conflict. ____

Consistency

- My communication remains stable under stress. ____
- I respond intentionally instead of impulsively. ____
- I focus on clarity over emotional release. ____
- I reinforce the same expectations over time. ____

TOTAL SCORE: ______

Score Reflection

72–90
Strong professional stability patterns are present.

54–71
Some consistency is present, but unstable patterns still appear under pressure.

36–53
Communication and response patterns may be unintentionally reinforcing instability.

Below 36
Reactive patterns may be affecting clarity, consistency, and workplace stability.

Reflection

Where do your lowest scores appear most often?

□ communication
□ expectations
□ boundaries
□ emotional response
□ consistency

What unstable pattern tends to repeat most often for you?

What response would stabilize that pattern next time?

Final Principle

Awareness is the starting point. Consistency is what change. When communication is unclear, expectations are not defined.
When expectations are not defined, assumptions replace clarity.

Section 3 — Expectations vs Assumptions

Most workplace conflict is not caused by poor intent.
It is caused by unspoken expectations and incorrect assumptions.

People often believe they are on the same page.
Many times, they are not.

The Core Problem

Expectations are often:

- assumed
- implied
- unclear
- never directly stated

Assumptions are then made to fill the gap.

The Result

- misalignment
- frustration
- repeated conflict

Expectation vs Assumption

Expectation

- clearly stated
- specific
- understood by both parties
- can be followed

Assumption

- not stated
- based on personal interpretation
- often incomplete
- leads to misunderstanding

Where This Shows Up

"I thought you were going to handle that."
"I assumed that was already done."
"You should have known."
"That's not what I meant."

These are not communication problems.
They are expectation failures.

The Pattern Loop

UNCLEAR EXPECTATION
↓
ASSUMPTION
↓
MISALIGNMENT
↓
FRUSTRATION
↓
REPEATED CONFLICT

What Stabilizes This

Clarity.

Not intention alone.
Not effort alone.
Not tone alone.

Professional Standard

If it is not clearly stated, it does not exist.

Expectation Control

Before moving forward, ask:

- Has this been clearly stated?
- Is this specific?
- Has the other person confirmed understanding?

If not, you are operating on assumption.

Examples

Unstable:
"I thought you knew what I meant."

Stable:
"Let me clarify exactly what I'm expecting."

Unstable:
"You should have told me."

Stable:
"Going forward, I need this communicated directly."

Expectation Reset Language

Use simple, repeatable language:

- "Let's clarify expectations."
- "Here's what I need moving forward."
- "Let's make sure we're aligned."
- "This is the expectation going forward."

Common Employee Mistake

Avoiding clarification to:

- keep the peace
- avoid tension
- not seem difficult
- avoid uncomfortable conversations

This does not prevent conflict.
It delays it.

Quick Check Tool

If you catch yourself thinking:

- "they should know"
- "I assumed"
- "I thought"

→ stop and clarify

Expectation Stability Model

Clear Expectation
↓
Shared Understanding
↓
Consistent Response
↓
Reduced Conflict

Under Pressure

When something goes wrong:

Do not:

- blame
- assume intent
- escalate emotionally

Instead:

- clarify what happened
- restate the expectation
- reset expectations moving forward

Examples in Practice

Miscommunication

Unstable:
"I already explained this. I don't know why this keeps happening."

Stable:
"Let's clarify expectations so this doesn't repeat."

Assumption

Unstable:
"I thought you were handling that."

Stable:
"Let's confirm who is responsible for this."

Boundary

Unstable:
"I'll just do it this time."

Stable:
"That falls outside my role. Let's clarify ownership."

Pressure

Unstable:
Responding emotionally under pressure

Stable:
"Let's slow this down and address it clearly."

Workplace Expectation Reflection

Think about a recent workplace frustration.

Answer:

1. What expectation existed?

2. Was it clearly stated?
   YES / NO

3. Was understanding confirmed?
   YES / NO

4. What assumption was made?

5. What response reinforced the confusion?

6. What could have clarified the expectation earlier?

7. What language could stabilize this moving forward?

Reset Statement

Clear expectations reduce assumptions.
Assumptions relace clarity.
Stability begins when expectations are directly communicated.

Closing
Once expectations are unclear, boundaries begin to break down.
This is where roles, responsibilities, and communication become unstable.

Section 4 — Professional Boundaries in Everyday Work

Workplace boundaries are not about being difficult.
They are about preventing instability.

When boundaries are unclear or inconsistent:

- patterns repeat
- workload increases
- resentment builds
- expectations become distorted

The Core Problem

Most employees do not struggle with knowing what is appropriate.
They struggle with consistently reinforcing it.

What Boundaries Actually Do

Boundaries:

- reduce emotional escalation
- define roles
- clarify responsibilities
- prevent overextension
- reduce confusion
- protect professional standards

Boundary vs No Boundary

No Boundary

- unclear roles
- overcommitment
- reactive responses
- repeated issues

Professional Boundary

- Stable expectations
- clear limits
- defined responsibilities
- consistent responses
- stable expectations

Where Boundaries Break Down

- saying yes when you should say no
- taking on work outside your role
- not addressing repeated behavior
- avoiding uncomfortable conversations
- changing your response depending on the person

These do not reduce problems.
They reinforce them.

The Pattern Loop

UNCLEAR BOUNDARY
↓
OVEREXTENSION
↓
FRUSTRATION
↓
INCONSISTENT RESPONSE
↓
REPEATED DEMAND

What Stabilizes Boundaries

Consistency.

Not intensity alone.
Not tone alone.
Not explanation alone.

Professional Standard

A boundary is not what you say once.
It is what you consistently reinforce.

Boundary Control Point

Before responding, ask:

- Is this within my role?
- Has this been clearly addressed before?
- Am I responding consistently?

If the answer is no, the boundary has not been established.

Examples

Unstable:
"Okay, I'll just take care of it this time..."

Stable:
"That falls outside my role. Let's clarify who owns this."

Unstable:
"I didn't want to say anything..."

Stable:
"This has come up before. We need to address it directly."

Boundary Language

Use simple, repeatable responses:

- "That's outside my role."
- "Let's clarify responsibility."
- "I'm not able to take that on."
- "We need to address this directly."
- "I'm going to keep this boundary consistent."

Micro Scripts — Boundary Reinforcement

When something is outside your role:
"That falls outside my role. Let's clarify ownership."

When work keeps getting added:
"I'm not able to take that on right now

. Let's review priorities."

When a boundary is ignored:
"This has come up before. I'm going to keep the boundary consistent."

When you feel pressure to say yes:
"I'm going to keep my current responsibilities aligned."

When expectations are unclear:
"Before I move forward, I need clarity on expectations."

Common Employee Mistake

Avoiding boundaries to:

- be helpful
- avoid conflict
- be liked
- Avoid disappointing people

This does not create stability.
It creates dependency and confusion.

Quick Check Tool

If you are:

- overexplaining → simplify
- apologizing unnecessarily → stop
- saying yes repeatedly → reassess
- feeling resentful → a boundary is missing

Boundary Stability Model

CLEAR BOUNDARY
↓
CONSISTENT RESPONSE
↓
PREDICTABLE EXPECTATION
↓
REDUCED OVERLOAD

Under Pressure

When boundaries are challenged:

Do not:

- justify excessively
- change your response
- avoid the conversation

Instead:

- restate the boundary
- keep it clear
- repeat it if necessary

Additional Indicators

If you are:

- feeling resentful → a boundary is missing
- consistent overexplaining → a boundary is weak
- repeatedly saying yes → a boundary is not reinforced
- avoiding conversation → a boundary is not set

When boundaries are not maintained, emotional responses increase. This is where consistency is most often lost.

Boundary Reflection Exercise

Think about a situation that repeatedly frustrates you at work.

1. What boundary may be unclear?

2. Where have your responses been inconsistent?

3. Are you overexplaining, avoiding, or changing your response?

4. What response keeps reinforcing the issue?

5. What clear boundary statement could stabilize this?

6. What response will you repeat consistently moving forward?

Boundary Reset

Boundaries are not maintained through emotion.

They are maintained through consistency.

Clear boundaries reduce confusion.

Consistent boundaries reduce instability.

Closing

Boundaries are not about control.
They are about consistency.

If you do not define and reinforce them,
the workplace will define them for you.

Section 5 — Emotional Regulation at Work

Emotions are part of every workplace.
They are not the problem.

The Core Problem

Most employees do not struggle with having emotions.
They struggle with responding to them under pressure.

What Happens Under Pressure

When stress increases:

- assumptions increase
- reactions become faster
- tone changes
- communication shifts
- consistency breaks

This is where patterns are reinforced.

Emotional Reaction vs Professional Response

Emotional Reaction

- immediate
- impulsive
- driven by feeling
- inconsistent

Professional Response

- repeatable
- controlled
- intentional
- measured
- consistent

Where Emotional Instability Shows Up

- reacting defensively
- raising tone
- shutting down
- overexplaining
- avoiding the situation

These responses do not resolve problems.
They reinforce them.

The Pattern Loop

TRIGGER
↓
EMOTIONAL REACTION
↓
ESCALATION
↓
LOSS OF CONTROL
↓
REPEATED PATTERN

What Stabilizes Emotional Response

Pause.

Not suppression.
Not avoidance.
Controlled response.

Professional Standard

You are responsible for your response—regardless of the situation.

Emotional Control Point

Before responding, ask:

- What am I reacting to?
- Is this helping or escalating the situation?
- What response will stabilize this?

If the response is emotional, it will likely reinforce the pattern.

Examples

Unstable:
"That's not fair, you're not listening to me."

Stable:
"Let's slow this down and clarify what's happening."

Unstable:
Silence, avoidance, or disengagement

Stable:
"I need a moment. I'll come back to this."

Emotional Regulation Tools

- pause before responding
- slow your pace
- lower your tone
- simplify your message

Control is not about removing emotion.
It is about managing how it is expressed.

Common Employee Mistake

Believing that:

- expressing emotion immediately = honesty
- reacting emotionally = authenticity
- reacting quickly = being real

In reality:
immediate reactions often escalate instability.

Quick Check Tool

If you are:

- reacting quickly → pause
- raising your tone → reset
- feeling overwhelmed → slow down
- avoiding the situation → re-engage

Emotional Stability Model

PAUSE
↓
CONTROLLED RESPONSE
↓
CLEAR COMMUNICATION
↓
REDUCED ESCALATION

Under Pressure

When emotions rise:

Do not:

- Over-explain emotionally
- match intensity
- respond immediately
- escalate tone

Instead:

- pause
- regulate
- respond intentionally

Emotional Response Reflection

Think about a recent workplace situation where emotions escalated.

1. What triggered your reaction?

2. What was your immediate response?

3. Did your response stabilize or escalate the situation?

4. Did you react quickly, avoid, over-explain, or become defensive?

5. What would a more controlled professional response have looked like?

6. What response could you repeat consistently moving forward?

Emotional Reset

Before responding:

- pause
- regulate
- simplify
- respond intentionally

Emotional stability is not about suppressing emotion.
It is about maintaining control under pressure.

Closing

Emotional control is not about being perfect.
It is about being consistent.

When your response remains stable, the situation becomes easier to manage.

Even when the other person remains inconsistent

Transition

When communication, expectations, and boundaries are unstable, situations become more difficult.

This is where patterns repeat most clearly.

Section 6 — Handling Difficult Workplace Situations

Difficult situations are not the exception in the workplace.
They are part of it.

The issue is not that they occur.
It is how they are handled.

The Core Problem

Most employees approach difficult situations reactively.

They:

- avoid
- overreact
- escalate
- overexplain

This does not resolve the situation.
It reinforces it.

Avoidance and inconsistency often become the pattern itself.

What Makes a Situation "Difficult"

Situations become difficult when:

- communication is unclear
- expectations are not aligned
- emotions are elevated
- boundaries are not reinforced

These are pattern issues—not isolated problems.

Common Types of Difficult Situations

- repeated miscommunication
- unclear ownership of tasks
- someone overstepping boundaries
- passive-aggressive behavior
- avoidance or lack of follow-through
- tension between coworkers

The Pattern Loop

DIFFICULT EVENT
↓
EMOTIONAL OR AVOIDANT RESPONSE
↓
ESCALATION OR DELAY
↓
NO RESOLUTION
↓
REPEATED SITUATION

What Stabilizes Difficult Situations

Clarity.
Consistency.
Direct response.

Professional Standard

Address the situation directly.
Do not delay.
Do not avoid.

Response Structure

Use a simple, repeatable approach:

1. Identify the issue
2. Clarify what is happening
3. State the expectation
4. Maintain the response

Examples

Unstable:
"I don't want to make this a big deal..."

Stable:
"This has come up a few times. Let's address it directly."

Unstable:
Ignoring the issue and hoping it improves

Stable:
"I want to clarify expectations, so this doesn't continue."

Key Distinction

Avoidance delays problems.
Direct response stabilizes them.

Micro Scripts — Difficult Situations

- "I want to address this directly, so it doesn't continue."
- "This has come up multiple times. Let's resolve it clearly.
- "I'd like to bring this back so we can address it."
- "I want to make sure we're aligned before moving forward."
- "Let's slow this down and keep it clear."

When to Stop Engaging

Not every situation improves with more communication.
Not every interaction benefits from continued engagement.

Some patterns continue because they are repeatedly engaged with each other.

Most employees believe:

- if I explain it better
- if I say it differently
- if I try one more time

→ the situation will improve

In many cases, it does not.

Repeated explanation without change often reinforces the cycle.

What This Looks Like

- repeated conversations with no change
- explaining the same point multiple times
- restating expectations without follow-through
- responding to the same behavior without resolution

At this point, the issue is no longer clarity.
It is repetition.

Professional Standard

Consistency does not always mean continuing to engage.
It means maintaining the same response without increasing effort.

What to Do Instead

Consistency matters more than finding the perfect wording

- state the expectation clearly
- respond once
- do not over-explain
- do not repeat unnecessarily
- document if the pattern continues
- escalate if appropriate

Quick Check

- Have I already stated this clearly?
- Has this been repeated without change?
- Am I continuing to engage out of frustration or habit?

Reset

Say it clearly.
Stop repeating it.
Maintain your response.
Allow the pattern to surface.

Common Employee Mistake

Waiting for:

- the right moment
- the right tone
- the right conditions

That moment rarely comes.

Quick Check Tool

If you are:

- avoiding → address it
- waiting → clarify now
- overthinking → simplify
- hoping it changes → intervene

Stabilization Model

DIRECT RESPONSE
↓
CLEAR EXPECTATION
↓
CONSISTENT FOLLOW-UP
↓
RESOLUTION OR STABILITY

Under Pressure

When a situation becomes uncomfortable:

Do not:

- withdraw
- escalate emotionally
- overexplain

Instead:

- stay direct
- stay clear
- stay consistent
- Avoid emotional escalation

Closing

Difficult situations do not resolve on their own.
They repeat until they are addressed directly and consistently.

Real Workplace Scenarios — Applying the Method

The goal is not to explain situations.
The goal is to respond to them consistently.

Unclear Responsibility

Unstable:
"I'll just take care of it."

Stable:
"Let's clarify who is responsible for this moving forward."

Repeated Miscommunication

Unstable:
"I already explained this."

Stable:
"This has come up multiple times. Let's clarify expectations so it doesn't continue."

Boundary Being Crossed

Unstable:
"Okay, I'll do it."

Stable:
"That falls outside my role. Let's clarify ownership."

Emotional Conversation

Unstable:
Matching tone or becoming defensive

Stable:
"Let's slow this down and address it clearly."

Pressure to Respond Quickly

Unstable:
Reacting immediately

Stable:
"I'm going to take a moment and respond clearly."

Workload Overload

Unstable:
Continuing to accept tasks

Stable:
"I'm not able to take that on. Let's clarify priorities."

Being Overlooked or Ignored

Unstable:
Staying silent or disengaging

Stable:
"I want to make sure this is clearly addressed."

Pattern Repeating Without Change

Unstable:
Ignoring it or becoming frustrated

Stable:
"This has continued despite being addressed. I want to bring this forward so we can resolve it."

Workplace Response Reflection

Think about a difficult workplace situation you are currently experiencing or have experienced recently.

1. What made the situation difficult?

2. Did you:
- avoid it
- overexplain
- react emotionally
- delay the conversation
- repeat yourself excessively

3. What expectation was unclear or not reinforced?

4. What would a more stable response have looked like?

5. Which response from this section could have helped stabilize the situation?

Reset Reminder

You do not need:
- the perfect tone
- the perfect timing
- the perfect wording

You need:
- clarity
- consistency
- direct response

Final Principle

Consistency matters more than the situation. The situation will change.
Your response should not.

Transition

Difficult situations become more unstable under pressure.
This is where consistency either breaks—or is reinforced.

Section 7 — Responding Under Pressure

Pressure is where most workplace patterns are reinforced.

Not during calm situations.
Not during planned conversations.
Under pressure.

Pressure Response Standard

Pause
Slow
Respond clearly
Stop

The Core Problem

Most employees know how to respond appropriately.
They just do not do it consistently when it matters.

What Happens Under Pressure

When pressure increases:

- responses become reactive
- communication becomes inconsistent
- boundaries weaken
- emotional control decreases

This is where stability breaks.

Under pressure, People Default To:

- Familiar reactions
- Emotional habits
- Automatic communication patterns
- Learned coping responses

Why This Matters

Your response under pressure determines:

- what gets reinforced
- what becomes normal
- what repeats

Reaction vs Response

Reaction

- immediate
- emotional
- inconsistent
- driven by pressure

Response

- controlled
- intentional
- consistent
- stable under pressure

The Pattern Loop

PRESSURE
↓
REACTIVE RESPONSE
↓
INCONSISTENCY
↓
REINFORCEMENT
↓
REPEATED INSTABILITY

What Stabilizes Response Under Pressure

Consistency.

Not intensity.
Not intention.

Professional Standard

Your response should not change based on pressure.

What Pressure Often Triggers

- urgency
- emotional reasoning
- Defensive communication
- Inconsistency

- Overexplaining
- Reactive decision-making

Response Control Point

Before responding under pressure, ask:

- Is this consistent with how I would normally respond?
- Am I reacting or responding?
- What outcome will this reinforce?

If the response changes under pressure, instability is reinforced.

Response Framework

Use a simple, repeatable sequence:

PAUSE
↓
ASSESS
↓
RESPOND CLEARLY
↓
STOP

Examples

Unstable:
Responding immediately with frustration or defensiveness

Stable:
"Let's slow this down and address it clearly."

Unstable:
Changing your response based on urgency or tone

Stable:
"I'm going to respond the same way I would in any situation."

Common Employee Mistake

Believing that pressure justifies:

- faster responses
- emotional reactions
- inconsistent behavior

It does not.

Pressure Does Not Justify:

- Reactive communication
- Emotional escalation
- Abandoning standards
- Inconsistent response

Pressure explains behavior.
It does not excuse it.

When You're the Only One Being Consistent

Consistency can feel ineffective when others are inconsistent.

You may notice:

- you are responding clearly, but others are not
- you are reinforcing expectations, but they continue to shift
- you are staying consistent, but the situation does not immediately improve

This does not mean the method is not working.
It means you are no longer reinforcing the pattern the way it depends on.

Most employees return to inconsistent responses at this point.

They:

- match the tone of others
- adjust communication based on frustration
- abandon consistency when it is not immediately effective

This restores the original pattern.

Professional Standard

Consistency is not dependent on others matching it.
It is maintained regardless of whether it is returned.

What This Requires

Continuing to:

- respond the same way
- communicate clearly
- reinforce expectations
- avoid reacting to inconsistency

Quick Check

- Am I abandoning consistency because others are inconsistent?
- Am I adjusting my response based on frustration?
- Am I expecting immediate change instead of reinforcing stability?

Reset

Return to the same response.
Repeat it.
Do not adjust it.

Quick Check Tool

If you are:

- rushing → pause
- reacting emotionally → reset
- changing your tone → stabilize
- abandoning your approach → return to it

Stability Model

CONSISTENT RESPONSE
↓
PREDICTABLE OUTCOME
↓
REINFORCED STABILITY
↓
REDUCED PRESSURE OVER TIME

Under Pressure

When pressure increases:

Do not:

- speed up your response
- match emotional intensity
- abandon your standards

Instead:

- slow down
- stay consistent
- respond intentionally

Closing

Pressure does not create new behavior.
It exposes existing patterns.

If your response remains consistent under pressure, stability follows.

Stability is maintained through repeated professional responses-especially under pressure.

Final Reinforcement

WHEN UNDER PRESSURE:

PAUSE
↓
SLOW DOWN
↓
RESPOND CLEARLY
↓
STOP

External patterns are only part of the system.
Internal patterns determine how you respond to them.

Pressure Response Reflection

Under Pressure, I Tend To:

Check any that apply:

- react quickly
- overexplain
- become defensive
- avoid the conversation
- shut down
- match tone or intensity
- change my communication style
- abandon boundaries
- rush to resolve discomfort
- repeat myself excessively
- become emotionally reactive
- withdraw from consistency
- take things personally
- over-accommodate
- stay silent instead of addressing issues

Pattern Awareness

1. What situations create the most pressure for me at work?

2. What changes in my communication when pressure increases?

3. What response patterns do I reinforce without realizing it?

4. What would a more stable response look like?

Consistency Reminder

Pressure does not create patterns.
It exposes them.

The goal is not perfection under pressure.
The goal is consistency.

Section 8 — Breaking Your Own Patterns at Work

Workplace patterns are not only external.
They are personal.

The Core Problem

Most employees recognize patterns in others.
They do not recognize the patterns they participate in.

What This Means

You are not just responding to workplace dynamics.
You are contributing to them.

Common Personal Patterns

- avoiding difficult conversations
- overexplaining
- needing immediate resolution
- reacting emotionally
- taking on too much
- not reinforcing boundaries
- changing responses under pressure

These patterns feel justified in the moment.
They become consistent over time.

The Pattern Loop

TRIGGER
↓
AUTOMATIC RESPONSE
↓
REINFORCEMENT
↓
REPEATED BEHAVIOR

Why This Matters

If your response stays the same, the pattern stays the same.

Professional Standard

You are responsible for identifying and changing your own patterns.

Personal Control Point

Before responding, ask:

- Is this how I usually respond?
- Has this created the same outcome before?
- What am I reinforcing right now?

If the response is automatic, the pattern will repeat.

What Actually Changes Patterns

Awareness is not enough.

Change requires:

- recognition
- interruption
- consistent new response

New responses feel uncomfortable before they feel natural.

Pattern Interruption Model

RECOGNIZE THE PATTERN
↓
INTERRUPT THE RESPONSE
↓
APPLY A DIFFERENT RESPONSE
↓
REPEAT CONSISTENTLY

Examples

Unstable:
Avoiding a conversation because it feels uncomfortable

Stable:
Addressing the issue directly and clearly

Unstable:
Overexplaining to justify your position

Stable:
Stating your point clearly and stopping

Common Employee Mistake

Believing:

- "This is just how I am"
- "This is how I handle things"

That mindset keeps patterns in place.

Patterns repeated long enough begin to feel like personality.

Quick Check Tool

If you notice:

- repeated frustration → pattern
- same conversations → pattern
- same outcome → pattern

→ change your response

Personal Stability Model

INTENTIONAL RESPONSE
↓
CONSISTENT APPLICATION
↓
NEW PATTERN
↓
IMPROVED OUTCOME

Under Pressure

When your usual pattern shows up:

Do not:

- default to habit
- justify the response
- ignore the pattern

Instead:

- recognize it
- interrupt it
- choose a different response

Closing

You cannot control every situation.
You can control how you participate in it.

When you change your response,
you change your pattern.

Personal Pattern Reflection

The Workplace Patterns I Most Recognize In Myself:

Check any that apply:

- avoiding uncomfortable conversations
- overexplaining
- reacting emotionally
- shutting down
- becoming defensive
- changing my tone under pressure
- abandoning boundaries
- rushing to fix situations
- taking responsibility for everything
- repeating conversations excessively
- tolerating repeated instability
- withdrawing instead of addressing issues
- matching emotional intensity
- needing immediate resolution

Pattern Awareness

1. What workplace situations trigger my usual patterns most often?

2. What response do I automatically default to?

3. What outcome does that response repeatedly create?

4. What professional response would interrupt that pattern?

Consistency Reminder

You do not change patterns by recognizing them once.

You change them by interrupting them repeatedly.

Section 9 — Protecting Yourself While Staying Professional

Why Protection Matters

This method is not about fixing the workplace.
It is about stabilizing your position within it.

Not every environment will improve.
Some will remain inconsistent.
Some individuals will not change.

The purpose is not to control those outcomes.

It is to ensure your responses remain:

- clear
- consistent
- professionally aligned

Regardless of the environment.

What This Does

When your responses remain consistent, you reduce:

- misinterpretation
- unnecessary escalation
- repeated involvement in the same issues

This does not mean the situation immediately improves.

It means your role within it becomes:

- more stable
- more predictable
- less reactive

The Responsibility Shift

You are not responsible for correcting the system.
You are not responsible for over-functioning to compensate for instability.

You are responsible for not reinforcing the patterns within it.

That is where protection begins.

The Core Problem

Many employees confuse professionalism with compliance.

They:

- say yes when they should not
- avoid speaking up
- tolerate repeated patterns
- adjust themselves to instability

This does not create stability.
It creates vulnerability.

What Professional Protection Actually Means

Professional protection is:

- clear communication
- consistent boundaries
- documented patterns
- controlled responses

Not:

- emotional reaction
- escalation
- avoidance

Protecting Yourself Without Escalating

Employees often believe they must choose between:

- staying silent
- escalating immediately

Both create problems.
Silence reinforces the pattern.

Unstructured escalation creates conflict.

There is a third option:

Consistent, structured response.

What This Looks Like

Instead of reacting:

- clarify expectations
- reinforce boundaries
- document patterns
- repeat your response

No escalation.
No avoidance.
No emotional reaction.

Professional Standard

Protection should not feel aggressive.
It should feel consistent.

Quick Check

- Am I staying silent to avoid making this worse?
- Am I reacting emotionally instead of responding clearly?
- Am I escalating without first being consistent?

Reset

Clarify
State expectation
Reinforce
Document if needed
Repeat

Protection vs Overreaction

Overreaction

- emotional escalation
- defensiveness
- impulsive response

Professional Protection

- clear
- direct
- documented
- consistent

Where Employees Get Stuck

“I don’t want to make this worse”
“I don’t want to seem difficult”
“I’ll just handle it”

These responses reinforce the pattern.

The Protection Breakdown

UNCLEAR EXPECTATION
↓
OVERCOMPLIANCE
↓
REPEATED DEMAND
↓
FRUSTRATION
↓
NO CHANGE

What Actually Protects You

Consistency + clarity + documentation

Professional Protection Model

CLARIFY
↓
SET BOUNDARY
↓
DOCUMENT PATTERN
↓
REPEAT RESPONSE

Examples

Unprotected:
"I'll just take care of it so it doesn't become an issue."

Protected:
"That falls outside my role. I'm documenting this so we can clarify ownership."

Unprotected:
Staying silent when patterns repeat

Protected:
"This has come up multiple times. I want to address it directly."

Documentation

Documentation is not escalation.
It is protection.

Use it when:

- patterns repeat
- expectations are unclear
- boundaries are ignored

Micro Scripts — Professional Protection

- "I'm documenting this to ensure clarity moving forward."
- "This has been addressed and continues. I want to bring this forward so it can be handled consistently."
- "I want to ensure responsibilities remain clearly defined."
- "This pattern is continuing. I want to address it directly."
- "I'm going to keep the response consistent and documented."

Quick Protection Check

If you are:

- repeatedly frustrated → pattern
- doing work outside your role → boundary issue
- unclear on expectations → clarification needed
- avoiding documentation → risk increases

Under Pressure

Do not:

- overcompensate
- stay silent
- absorb the issue

Instead:

- clarify
- state expectation
- document
- repeat response

Workplace Defense Quick Guide

Workplace situations do not require different strategies.
They require consistent responses.

When you feel confused
→ clarify expectations
"Let's make sure we're aligned on what's expected."

When expectations are unclear
→ state it directly
"I want to clarify exactly what is expected moving forward."

When boundaries are crossed
→ reinforce clearly
"That falls outside my role. Let's clarify responsibility."

When communication becomes emotional
→ slow it down
"Let's take a step back and address this clearly."

When something keeps repeating
→ address the pattern
"This has come up multiple times. Let's address it directly."

When you feel pressured to react
→ pause
"I'm going to take a moment and respond clearly."

When you are doing too much
→ reset the boundary
"I'm not able to take that on. Let's clarify ownership."

When you are being overlooked
→ bring it back to clarity
"I want to make sure this is clearly addressed."

When you need to protect yourself
→ document and reinforce
"I'm documenting this so expectations are clear moving forward."

Final Principle

Do not change your response based on the situation.
Change the outcome by keeping your response consistent.

When Consistency Does Not Change The Pattern

Clarify
Respond
Reinforce
Document

If the pattern continues:
Escalate professionally.

When to Handle It Yourself vs When to Escalate

The Core Problem

Most employees struggle with knowing:

- when to address something directly
- when to involve leadership
- when to document and escalate

They either:

- avoid escalation completely
- escalate too quickly

Both create instability.

The Key Distinction

Not every issue should be escalated.
But repeated patterns should not be handled alone.

Handle It Yourself When:

- it is a first occurrence
- expectations are unclear
- it can be resolved directly
- no pattern has formed

Escalate When:

- the issue repeats
- expectations were already clarified
- boundaries are ignored
- behavior continues despite consistent response

The Escalation Pattern

ISSUE
↓
DIRECT RESPONSE
↓
REPEATED ISSUE
↓
NO CHANGE
↓
ESCALATION REQUIRED

What Escalation Is (and Is Not)

Escalation is:

- structured
- documented
- clear
- pattern-based

Escalation is not:

- emotional
- reactive
- blaming
- impulsive

Before Escalating

Confirm:

- expectations were clearly stated
- your response has been consistent
- the issue has repeated
- boundaries were reinforced

If not, address it directly first.

How to Escalate Professionally

Unstable:
"This keeps happening and nothing is being done."

Stable:
"This has come up multiple times. I've clarified expectations and addressed it directly, but the pattern continues. I want to bring this forward so we can address it consistently."

Documentation Before Escalation

Document:

- what happened
- when it happened
- what was communicated
- what response was given
- what repeated

This creates clarity and protects you.

Quick Decision Tool

- One-time issue → handle directly
- Repeated issue → escalate
- Expectations unclear → clarify first
- Response inconsistent → reset first

Under Pressure

Do not:

- escalate out of frustration
- escalate without clarity
- escalate without documentation

Instead:

- pause
- organize facts
- communicate clearly
- escalate based on pattern

Closing

Handling issues directly builds clarity.
Escalating patterns builds protection.

Knowing the difference creates stability.

Final System Reminder

Consistency in response determines:
what changes
and what repeats

Final Integration — Applying the Method at Work

The Daily Application Loop

Every workplace situation can be approached the same way.

1. **Recognize the pattern**
   What is repeating? What feels familiar?
2. **Clarify what is happening**
   Separate:

- facts
- assumptions
- expectations

3. **Respond clearly and directly**
   Focus on:

- clarity
- consistency
- reinforcement

4. **Repeat the same response**
   Stability is created through repetition—not variation.

This is not something you apply once.
It is how you approach situations consistently over time.

When this becomes automatic:

- communication stabilizes
- expectations become clearer
- repeated issues decrease

Not because everything changes.
Because your response does.

What This Book Provides

- recognition of patterns
- clear communication
- defined expectations
- consistent boundaries
- controlled responses under pressure

What Determines Results

Consistency.

Not effort.
Not intention.

The Cycle Breaker Method™ is applied through consistent response within the Workplace Pattern Cycle.

The System in Practice

RECOGNIZE THE PATTERN
↓
CLARIFY THE EXPECTATION
↓
RESPOND CONSISTENTLY
↓
REINFORCE THE RESPONSE

Application Standard

Use the same approach:

- across situations
- across people
- under pressure

What to Expect

At first:

- resistance
- discomfort
- inconsistency

Over time:

- clarity
- reduced conflict
- more predictable outcomes

Final Principle

Patterns do not change because you understand them.
They change because you respond differently—consistently.

Closing

You do not need to change everything at once.
You need to change what you reinforce.

That is how workplace stability is created.

REFLECTION

- What situation keeps repeating?
- How do I usually respond?
- What does this reinforce?
- What response would change this?
- How will I apply this consistently?

Stabilization Model

RECOGNIZE PATTERN
↓
CLARIFY EXPECTATION
↓
RESPOND CONSISTENTLY
↓
REINFORCE RESPONSE
↓
STABILIZE PATTERN

When patterns continue, protection becomes necessary.
This is where **consistency supports both clarity and stability.**

What gets reinforced becomes normal.

What becomes normal becomes culture.

Final Self-Check

What pattern shows up most often in your work?

What response have you been using?

What response will you use moving forward?

Final Page — Daily Use Reference

The Cycle Breaker Method™

**Workplace situations will change.
Your response should not.**

The Core Loop

Recognize
↓
Clarify
↓
Respond
↓
Reinforce

1. Recognize the Pattern

What is repeating?

- same confusion
- same tension
- same outcome

If it feels familiar, it is a pattern.

2. Clarify the Expectation

What needs to be clearly stated?

- What is expected?
- Who is responsible?
- What is unclear?

If it is not clearly stated, it does not exist.

3. Respond Clearly

Keep your response:

- clear
- direct
- neutral

Examples:

- “Let’s clarify expectations.”
- “I want to make sure we’re aligned.”
- “That falls outside my role.”

4. Reinforce the Response

Do not change your response next time.

Stability is created through repetition, not variation.

Under Pressure

Pause
↓
Slow down
↓
Respond clearly
↓
Stop

When Something Feels Off

- confusion → clarify
- frustration → boundary issue
- repetition → pattern
- pressure → stay consistent

Boundary Check

- Is this within my role?
- Has this been clearly addressed?
- Am I responding consistently?

If not, the boundary is not established.

Protection Check

- Is this repeating?
- Have I already clarified expectations?
- Do I need to document this?

Protection = clarity + consistency + documentation

Escalation Check

- One-time issue → handle directly
- Repeated issue → escalate
- No clarity → clarify first
- No consistency → reset first

Stop Engaging When Needed

- Said it clearly?
- Still repeating?

Say it once.
Do not over-explain.
Document if needed.

Final Standard

Do not change your response based on:

- pressure
- people
- tone
- situation

Change the situation by keeping your response consistent.

Final Principle

What gets reinforced becomes normal.

What becomes normal becomes culture.

Cycle Breaker Method™ Feedback

The Cycle Breaker Method™ is designed to be applied in real workplace situations.

If you've applied the method individually or within a team, feedback helps strengthen future development and application of the system.

Your experience helps strengthen the method and improve understanding of how it is applied across different workplace environments.

Submit your feedback at:

cyclebreakermethod.com/feedback

www.ingramcontent.com/pod-product-compliance
Lightning Source LLC
LaVergne TN
LVHW061253100826
845148LV00008B/1111

* 9 7 9 8 2 3 4 0 7 2 9 8 6 *